Contents

Teachers' notes	1
Donkeys	5
Missing numbers	6
Three in a line	7
Pattern game	8
Pattern game continued	9
Flowers	10
Balloons	11
Eggs	12
Apples	13
Crabs – 1	14
Crabs – 2	15
What comes next – 1	16
What comes next – 2	17
Telephones	18
Telephone numbers	19
Hedgehogs – 1	20
Hedgehogs – 2	21
Coloured rods	22
Add 1	23
Subtract 1	23
Number 10	24
One more	25
Two more	25
Number flaps	26
Street	27
Handful of cubes	28
Colouring numbers	29
9 buttons	30
My pattern	30
Take some away	31
Staircase	31
Dice patterns	32

Teachers' notes

Aims of this book
The aim of this book is to provide you with well-presented and mathematically valuable supplementary material which will link with your existing scheme of work for mathematics, and which children will enjoy using. To help you make the best use of the activities, please read the following notes.

Printing
Although photocopying on to white paper may be the simplest way for you to copy the activities in this book, do consider other alternatives. Some pages benefit from copying directly on to card; some look much more interesting when printed on coloured paper or card. If your school does not have the facilities to do this, you may be able to make copies using a duplicator or a printing machine at a larger primary or secondary school close to you, or perhaps at a teachers' centre.

To keep reusable cards or worksheets in good condition, you could put them inside plastic wallets, laminate them or cover then with clear sticky plastic. Even copies made on paper, rather than card, are surprisingly strong when covered.

Record keeping and storage
We have not provided a separate system of record keeping for these activities, as most teachers prefer to add to their existing scheme of records. You could use the child's own maths writing book to make a note of activities used.

Worksheets can usually be fastened into the child's book with a piece of sticky tape, like an extra page in the book, to act as an obvious reminder of an activity completed.

Mathematical content
This book provides activities which help children to continue patterns with objects and numbers, and to make up patterns of their own. They are encouraged to explore and use patterns in addition and subtraction facts for totals up to 10, and to recognise odd and even numbers.

Practical work in an understandable context is used to introduce the idea of a 'missing number' and of representing a missing number with a symbol. Children are also given the opportunity to make up their own questions and puzzles for each other.

Each activity needs introducing by the teacher if children are to make the most of it. A few minutes spent discussing their work once they have finished is also worthwhile. Sometimes, activities may be taken home to talk about with parents or other family members.

Notes on individual activities

Page 5: Donkeys
Children make up a number pattern by feeding the donkeys different numbers of carrots. There is an extra carrot in case one gets lost.

◆ ESSENTIALS FOR MATHS: First number patterns

Page 6: Missing numbers

This sheet can be used as it is or cut into strips. If you decide to use individual strips you will need to tell the children to put their names on each strip. They will also need to be familiar with the concept of zero.

The children will also enjoy following-up this activity by making their own strips with missing numbers for their friends or family to complete.

Page 7: Three in a line

Children have to fill in the missing number on each strip.

Pages 8 and 9: Pattern game

These two pages make a matching game for three children to play. Both pages should be photocopied on to card. The numbers on page 8 should be cut into 3 separate strips, one for each child. The bees on page 9 should be cut into 21 separate cards. The bee cards should then be placed upside-down on the table.

Each child takes it in turn to choose and look at a bee card and place it on their strip if it matches, or turn it back if it does not. The game continues until each child has completed their number strip.

This game can also be played with the bee cards being kept as three strips and the numbers cut into 21 small cards.

It is also possible to play this game using two copies of page 9 or with two copies of page 8. One must be cut into 3 strips while the other should be cut into 21 small card.

Page 10: Flowers

The children need to draw one flower in the square and then complete the sums. The sum could be completed with a number or a drawing of the flowers. The children then need to be encouraged to look for and talk about the pattern the answers produce.

Page 11: Balloons

Here children are working with addition facts for the number 6. Some children will be able to add up the balloons and write the sum next to the relevant child, for example: 3 + 3 = 6.

Page 12: Eggs

The 4 eggs can be placed in the egg box to produce a variety of different patterns. Some children may request a further sheet as they recognise other possibilities. The diagram opposite suggests some possible solutions.

Page 13: Apples

There should be 4 apples on each tree but some have been eaten. The children have to work out how many are missing and complete the sum. It may be helpful for some children to make little card apples with which to work.

Pages 14 and 15: Crabs

The children are using addition and subtraction facts for the number 5 as they have to find how many crabs are hiding behind the seaweed. The seaweed is being used as a symbol to represent the missing number of crabs. Children can reinforce this activity by going on to draw their own crabs and seaweed, cutting them out and actually placing the crabs under the seaweed. The children could also be asked to write down the number of crabs they can see and the number of crabs that are hiding as a sum.

Pages 16 and 17: What comes next?

Page 16 gives children an opportunity to look at and continue a repeating number pattern.

Page 17 provides an opportunity for children to invent their own number patterns. This sheet can be used for children to start a number pattern for their friends to continue.

Page 18: Telephones

Children may wish to compare the arrangement of numbers on a telephone with those on a calculator.

Page 19: Telephone numbers

Finding 4 telephone numbers that are easy to remember and 4 that are difficult to remember is a very subjective activity. Children usually include their own telephone number (if they know it) in the list of easy numbers to remember even though their friends may disagree. As businesses often try to choose telephone numbers that will be easy for their customers or clients to remember it is helpful for children to have a copy of the *Yellow Pages* or another commercial telephone directory.

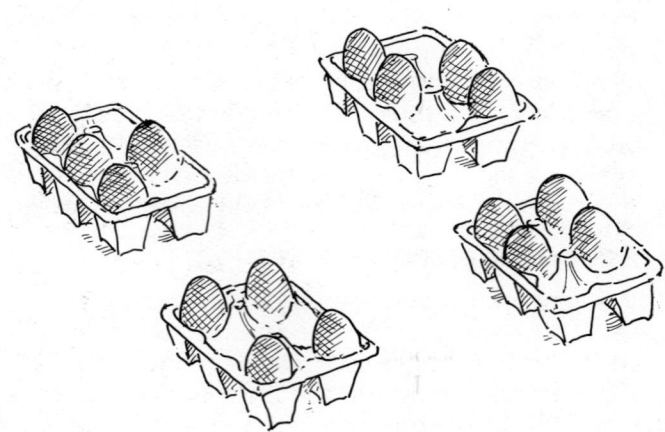

◆ ESSENTIALS FOR MATHS: First number patterns

Pages 20 and 21: Hedgehogs

On page 20 the children are asked to use addition facts for the number 8 as they have to find the number of hedgehogs that are asleep under the leaves.

On page 21 there are hedgehogs and piles of leaves for the children to make up further number patterns for the number 8. They may need more than one copy of this sheet. Children usually enjoy attaching the pile of leaves as a flap which can be lifted to reveal the hedgehogs underneath. Some children may need to join together two piles of leaves in order to cover their hedgehogs.

Page 22: Coloured rods

Children should work with interlocking cubes or coloured number rods. It is easier for them to identify and talk about the stepped pattern if they use 2 different colours, one for the cubes already on the sheet and the other colour for the cubes they draw themselves. This activity could be taken a stage further by asking the children to record the rods as a sum and identify the pattern.

Page 23: Add 1 and Subtract 1

This A4 sheet should be cut in half to make two A5 worksheets. With each sheet the children should be encouraged to talk about the pattern they produce. Some children may be able to produce their own similar number patterns.

Page 24: Number 10

Provide children with counters or something else that they can use for counting. Similar sheets could be made for other numbers.

Page 25: One more and Two more

This A4 sheet should be cut in half to make two A5 worksheets. The children have to look carefully at the pattern that is already there before they attempt to continue it. They usually find it easier if they say the pattern out loud. Some children may need help recognising that it is not the number of twos that they have to count but the total when they are added together.

You may like each child to write their name on the back of the number flap sheets.

Page 26: Number flaps

This is an introduction to even numbers. Children need scissors to cut along the dotted lines. They then need to fold down the flaps with the stars.

This reveals the even numbers. This can be a purely practical activity or children can record the even numbers on the sheet or elsewhere. They can also be asked to find the odd numbers or make other patterns.

Page 27: Street

Children fold the houses to stand up in order to make the street. This enables them to see the houses actually opposite each other. Children can then number the doors, as most streets are numbered, with odd numbers on one side and even numbers on the other. Children could start with 1, or those with more confidence could start with a larger number. They can then colour in their streets.

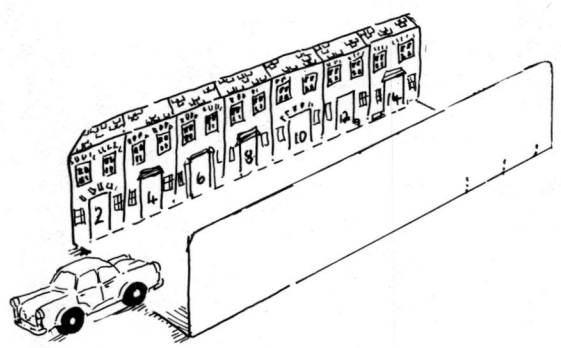

Some children may be able to number a further street in a different pattern, for example, up one side and down the other.

◆ ESSENTIALS FOR MATHS: First number patterns

Page 28: Handful of cubes
The children may want to try this several times to investigate different numbers of cubes.

Page 29: Colouring numbers
The children have to look for the even numbers carefully as the patterns produced in each block are not the same. Compulsive colourers need to be told that only some of the squares are going to be coloured in!

Pages 30 and 31 provide you with 4 separate activities on A5 workcards.

Page 30: 9 buttons
This game is good practice of addition facts for the number 9. Children do need to be told that they must include all the buttons in one or other of the boxes. Similar games could be made for different numbers and other containers can be substituted for the boxes.

Page 30: My pattern
Although the illustration shows children using interlocking cubes in towers, when they become familiar with this game they usually produce interesting shapes as well as more adventurous number patterns.

Page 31: Take some away
The numbers can be altered to suit the children in your class. Children may need to be reminded that they must take the same number of cubes from each card.

Page 31: Staircase
The children need to work with interlocking cubes. The staircase pattern is much more obvious if each child uses 15 cubes of the same colour but different from their friends. They could go on to investigate other triangular numbers that will make staircases and then join them together to make rectangles.

Page 32: Dice patterns
Children always enjoy working with dice. They may be able to record their findings as sums and discover for themselves that the opposite sides of a dice, when added together, make 7.

National Curriculum: Maths

In addition to the relevant programmes of study in AT1, the following PoS from AT3 are relevant to the activities in this book:

Pupils should engage in activities which involve:

Level 1
- copying, continuing and devising repeating patterns represented by objects/apparatus or single-digit numbers.

Level 2
- exploring and using patterns in addition and subtraction facts to 10.
- distinguishing odd and even numbers.
- understanding the use of a symbol to stand for an unknown number.

Scottish 5-14 Curriculum: Mathematics

Attainment outcome	Strand	Attainment target	Level
Number, money and measurement	Range and type of numbers	Work with whole numbers 0 to 20. Count and order.	A
	Patterns and sequences	Work with simple patterns 1 to 10. Copy, continue and describe simple patterns.	A
	Patterns and sequences	Even and odd numbers.	B
	Add and subtract	Add mentally for numbers 0 to 10.	A
	Functions and equations	Find the missing numbers in statements where symbols are used for unknown numbers.	B
Information handling	Collect	By collecting information about familiar objects.	A
Shape, position and movement	Position and movement	Discuss position and movement associated with position of object; above, below.	A

◆ ESSENTIALS FOR MATHS: First number patterns

◆ Name _____

Donkeys O|♡∨d

Colour in the carrots and feed the donkeys. Give each big donkey 2 carrots. Give each little donkey 1 carrot.

◆ ESSENTIALS FOR MATHS: First number patterns

5

◆ Name _____

Missing numbers

Fill in the missing numbers.

| 0, 1, 2, 3, [4], 5, 6, [7], 8, 9 |
| 5, 6, [7], 8, 9, [10], 11, 12 |
| 8, 7, [6], 5, 4, 3, [2], 1, [0] |
| 7, 6, [5], 4, [3], 2, [1], 0 |
| 10, [9], 8, [7], 6, 5, [4], 3 |

◆ Name _____

Three in a line

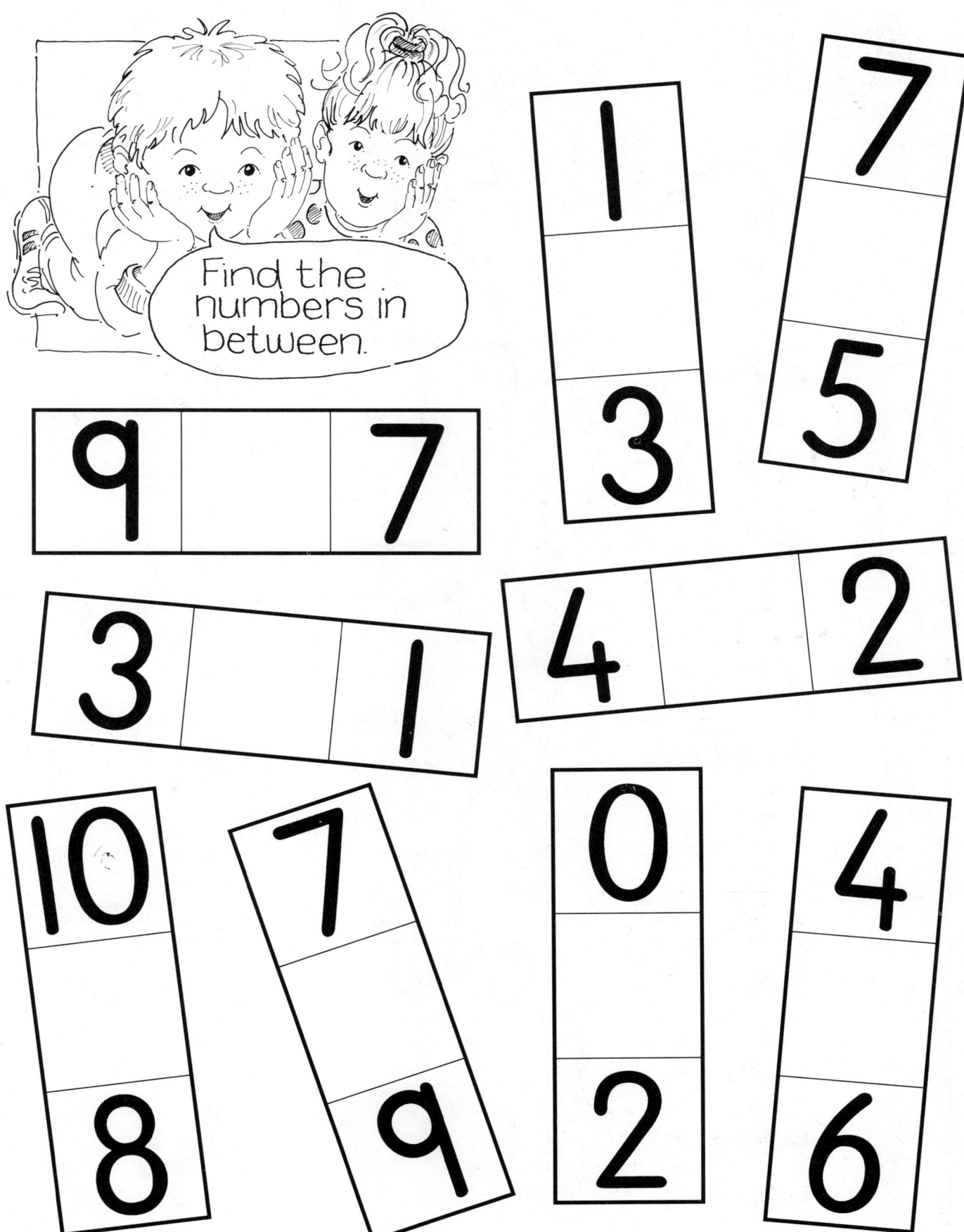

◆ ESSENTIALS FOR MATHS: First number patterns

Pattern game

1	2	1	2	1	2	1
3	4	3	4	3	4	3
5	6	5	6	5	6	5

◆ ESSENTIALS FOR MATHS: First number patterns

Pattern game continued

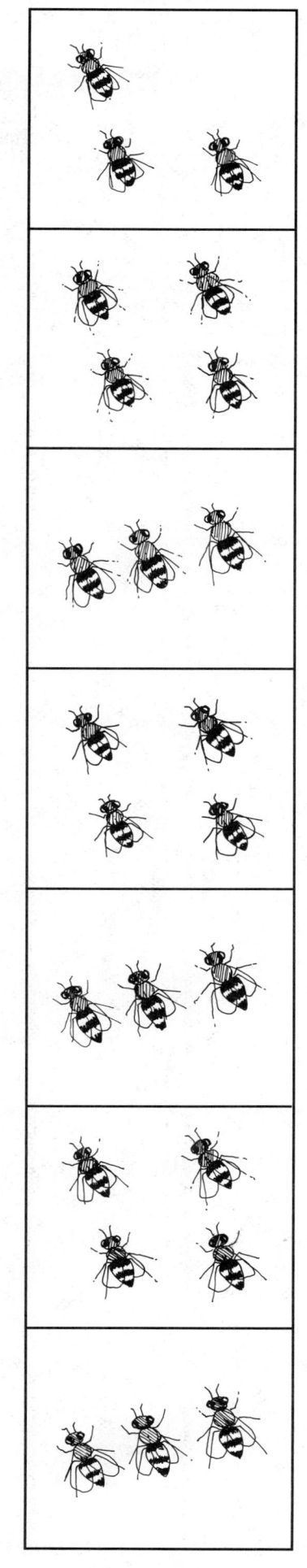
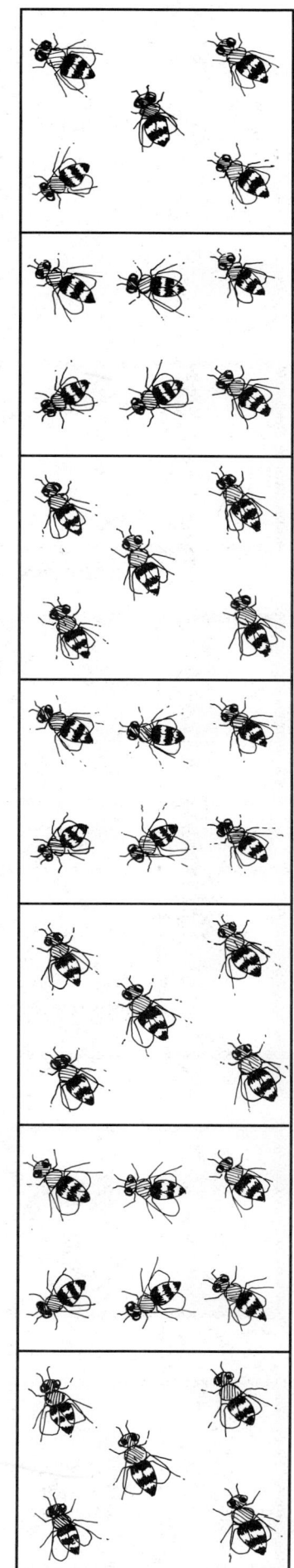

◆ ESSENTIALS FOR MATHS: First number patterns

◆ Name _____

Flowers

Draw 1 flower in each square and finish the sums.

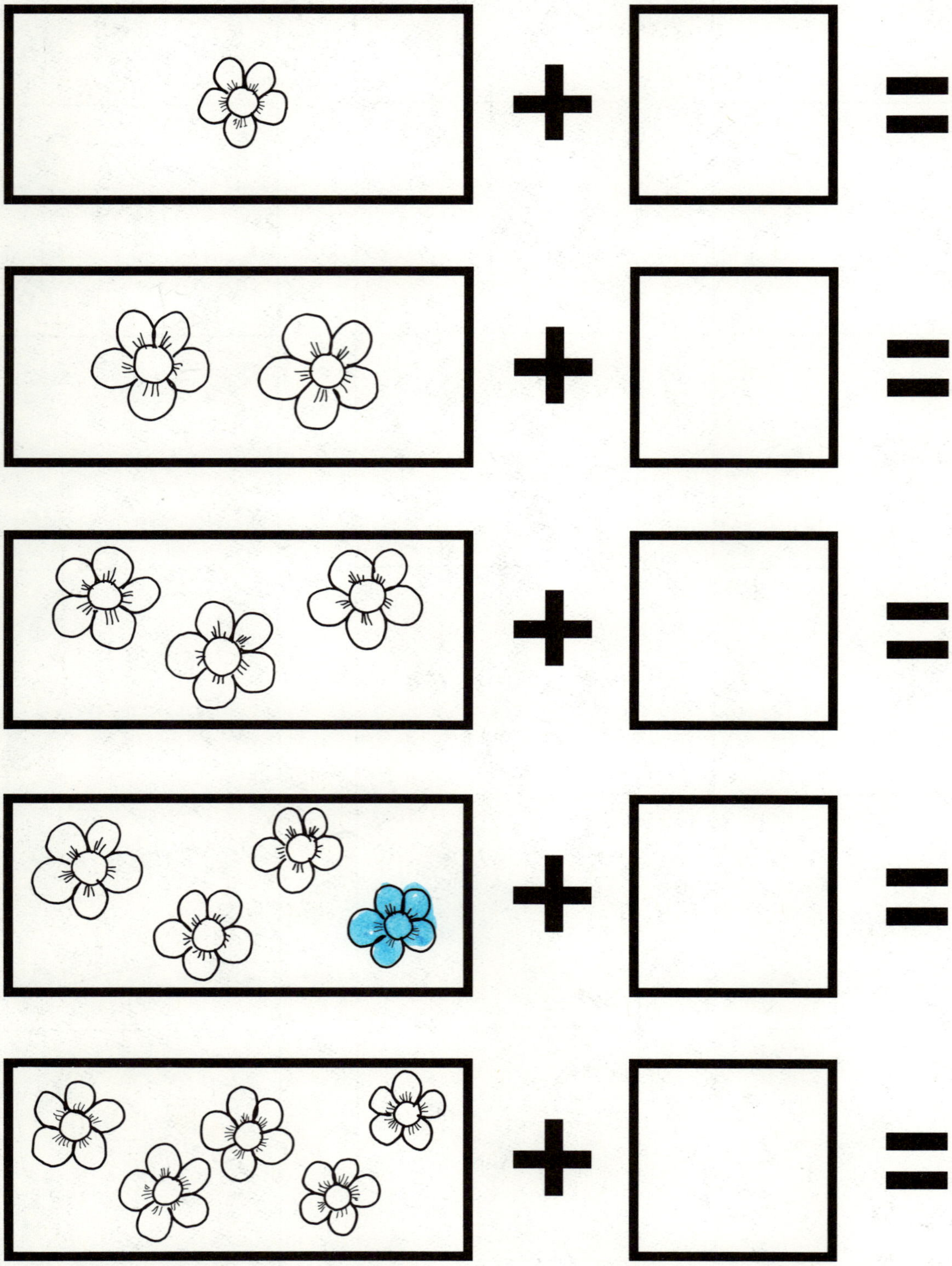

 +  =

 +  =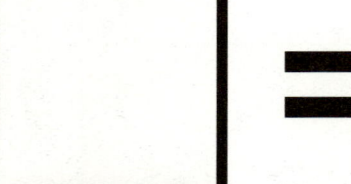

 +  =

 +  =

◆ ESSENTIALS FOR MATHS: First number patterns

10

◆ Name _____

Balloons

Colour my balloons blue.

Colour my balloons green.

Colour my balloons red.

Draw longer strings so that each child has 6 balloons.

◆ ESSENTIALS FOR MATHS: First number patterns

◆ Name _____

Eggs

Draw 4 eggs in each box. How many different patterns can you find?

◆ ESSENTIALS FOR MATHS: First number patterns

12

◆ Name _____

Apples

There used to be 4 apples on each tree. Colour in the apples and find out how many have been eaten.

4 − ☐ = 2

4 − ☐ = 1

4 − ☐ = 3

4 − ☐ = 4

◆ ESSENTIALS FOR MATHS: First number patterns

◆ Name _____

Crabs – 1

There are 5 crabs in each picture but some have crawled under the seaweed.

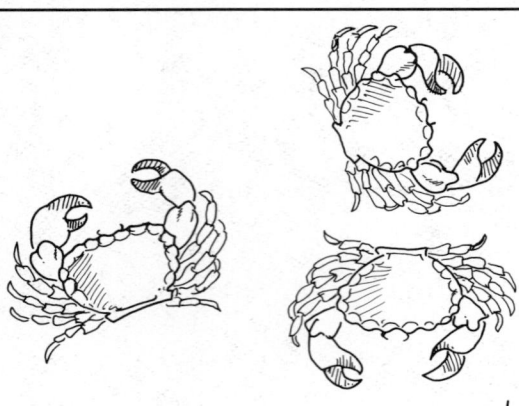 

How many are hiding? ☐

How many are hiding? ☐

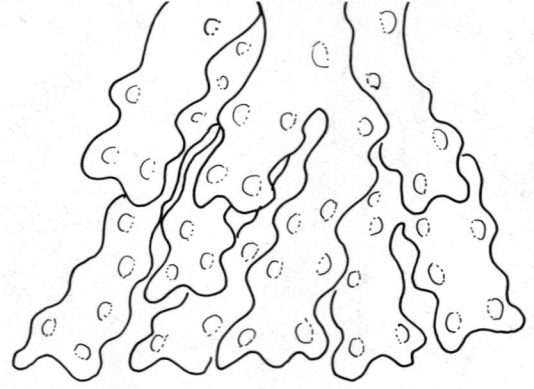 

How many are hiding? ☐

◆ ESSENTIALS FOR MATHS: First number patterns 14

◆ Name _____

Crabs – 2

There are 5 crabs in each picture but some have crawled under the seaweed.

How many are hiding? ☐

How many are hiding? ☐

How many are hiding? ☐

◆ ESSENTIALS FOR MATHS: First number patterns

◆ Name _____

What comes next – 2

Make up number patterns of your own.

◆ ESSENTIALS FOR MATHS: First number patterns

◆ Name _____

Telephones

Fill in the missing numbers.

◆ Name _____

Hedgehogs – 1

There are 8 hedgehogs in each picture but some are still asleep under the leaves. How many are asleep?

[hedgehogs] + [leaves] = 8

___ are asleep.

[leaves] + [hedgehogs] = 8

___ are asleep.

[hedgehog] + [leaves] = 8

___ are asleep.

◆ ESSENTIALS FOR MATHS: First number patterns
20

◆ Name _____

Hedgehogs – 2

Colour in and cut out the hedgehogs and piles of leaves. Now use them to make some sums that make 8.

◆ ESSENTIALS FOR MATHS: First number patterns

21

◆ Name _____

Coloured rods

Draw extra cubes so that there are 7 in each row. Use real cubes to help you.

◆ ESSENTIALS FOR MATHS: First number patterns   22

◆ Name ───────────

Subtract 1

Do the sums and then look at the pattern the numbers make.

1 - 1 =
2 - 1 =
3 - 1 =
4 - 1 =
5 - 1 =
6 - 1 =
7 - 1 =
8 - 1 =
9 - 1 =
10 - 1 =

◆ ESSENTIALS FOR MATHS: First number patterns

◆ Name ───────────

Add 1

Do the sums and then look at the pattern the numbers make.

1 + 1 =
2 + 1 =
3 + 1 =
4 + 1 =
5 + 1 =
6 + 1 =
7 + 1 =
8 + 1 =
9 + 1 =
10 + 1 =

◆ ESSENTIALS FOR MATHS: First number patterns

23

◆ Name _____

Number 10

"Fill in the spaces and look at the pattern."

"Use 10 counters to help you."

10 + ☐ = 10
9 + ☐ = 10
8 + ☐ = 10
7 + ☐ = 10
6 + ☐ = 10
5 + ☐ = 10
4 + ☐ = 10
3 + ☐ = 10
2 + ☐ = 10
1 + ☐ = 10
0 + ☐ = 10

◆ ESSENTIALS FOR MATHS: First number patterns

◆ Name _____

One more

1
1 + 1 =
1 + 1 + 1 =
1 + 1 + 1 + 1 =
1 + 1 + 1 + 1 + 1 =

◆ ESSENTIALS FOR MATHS: First number patterns

◆ Name _____

Two more

2
2 + 2 =
2 + 2 + 2 =
2 + 2 + 2 + 2 =

◆ ESSENTIALS FOR MATHS: First number patterns

Number flaps

◆ Cut along the dotted lines. Put the flaps down with the * on.

*	*	*	*	*

Fold

1 2 3 4 5 6 7 8 9

Fold

◆ What numbers can you see now?

◆ Name _____

◆ ESSENTIALS FOR MATHS: First number patterns

26

◆ Name _____

Street

◆ ESSENTIALS FOR MATHS: First number patterns

◆ Name _____

Handful of cubes

 "Pick up a handful of cubes and guess whether you have an odd or an even number."

"Now match the cubes in pairs, if there is one left over you have an odd number."

 "Draw your cubes here."

"Did you have an odd number of cubes? _____"

Colouring numbers

Colour in all the even numbers.

1	2	3	4
5	6	7	8
9	10	11	12
13	14	15	16
17	18	19	20

1	2
3	4
5	6
7	8
9	10
11	12
13	14
15	16
17	18
19	20

1	2	3	4	5
6	7	8	9	10
11	12	13	14	15
16	17	18	19	20

Look at the patterns you have made.

Take some away

Staircase